Daily Sparks

30-Day Devotional

Volume 1

Tyler Jaynes

Copyright © 2023 Tyler Jaynes

All rights reserved.

ISBN: 9798860795167

Cover Design: Tyler Jaynes

Editors:
Jogust Productions
Terry L. Jaynes
Candice M. Castro

FOREWORD

Tyler Jaynes' book, *Daily Sparks, Vol. 1*, is a fresh reminder that dynamite still comes in small packages.

His unique insight into the scriptures reveals a solid scriptural knowledge and a wisdom that is well beyond his years that is sorely needed in today's culture.

Regardless of your age, Tyler's first 30-Day Devotional is sure to build your faith in God's Word and inspire you in your walk with the Lord.

Get ready to be ignited by the power of the Holy Spirit as you do a deep dive daily to begin flinging a few sparks of your own.

-Pastor Cathy Duplantis
Jesse Duplantis Ministries,
Covenant Church

INTRODUCTION

Thank you for taking the time with this book. You are making a wise investment of your time! Take whatever resonates with you in these devotionals and bring it into your prayer, meditation, and personal conversations with God.

If something is speaking to you, it's connecting with you for a reason! Even if it's just one concept or idea that stands out, revisit it often. These devotions are meant to be a catalyst to set your mind on a path for the Holy Spirit to continue on.

I give you FULL PERMISSION to use the space in this book to highlight and write whatever thoughts or ideas stand out to you. This book can be a catalyst, but the Holy Spirit IN YOU will engrave these words onto your heart.

It just takes ONE SPARK to catch and set your life on a new course!

CONTENTS

Daily Sparks

30-Day Devotional

Volume 1

Day 1
NOW IS THE TIME

There comes a time in your life when you just know that NOW is the time!

It's not going to get easier.
YOU are going to have to get stronger.

"Be strong... and WORK, for I am with you,"
declares the Lord Almighty in Haggai 2:4 (NIV).

God Himself is GIVING you the strength to expand in new ways.

He's granting you a supernatural ability to do what you couldn't do before.

Now it's time to go to work!

-

Self-Reflective Questions:

What areas do I sense that "NOW is the time" to take steps forward in?

If I KNEW the strength of God would back me as I stepped out, what BIGGER things would I reach for?

Related Scriptures:

Haggai 2:4 (NIV)
"'Be strong, all you people of the land,' declares the LORD, **'and work. For I am with you,'** declares the LORD Almighty."

Hebrews 11:1 (NIV)
"**Now** faith is **confidence** in what we hope for and **assurance** about what we do not see."

Joshua 1:5-6 (BSB)
"No one shall stand against you all the days of your life. As I was with Moses, so will I be with you; I will never leave you nor forsake you. **Be strong and courageous**, for you shall give these people the inheritance of the land that I swore to their fathers I would give them."

PERSONAL NOTES:

Day 2
GET FIRM

I often find myself waiting on something that's been waiting on me.

It's like waiting on your waiter while your waiter is waiting on you... Nothing will happen, and you will remain hungry!

Then comes the typical religious thought: "Maybe God's trying to teach me something?"

NOPE!
You've just been stuck wavering back and forth and need to get FIRM!

Get concrete so long OVERDUE things can start moving INTO PLACE for you.

A man pleading for results:
"Jesus, if you can do anything, help!"

Jesus' response:
"What do you mean, 'If I can?' If YOU can believe, anything is possible!"

God is basically saying, "YOU get firm about this; I'm backing your decision!"

Related Scriptures:

Mark 9:22-24 (NLT)
"Have mercy on us and help us, if you can." "**What do you mean, 'If I can'?**" Jesus asked. "**Anything is possible if a person believes**." The father instantly cried out, "I do believe, but help me overcome my unbelief."

Luke 17:6 (NIV)
"He replied, "**If you have faith** as small as a mustard seed, you can say to this mulberry tree, 'Be uprooted and planted in the sea,' and it will obey you."

James 2:26 (BLB)
"...**faith apart from works is dead**."

James 1:6-7 (NIV)
"But when you ask, **you must believe and not doubt**, because the one who doubts is like a wave of the sea, blown and tossed by the wind. That person should not expect to receive anything from the Lord."

PERSONAL NOTES:

Day 3
KEEPING YOURSELF ENCOURAGED

Keeping yourself encouraged is a full-time job.

The last person who needs to be against you...
is YOU.

Refuse to beat yourself up!
There are enough things in life that attempt to do
that already!

Yes, accept responsibility and make corrections.
Then MOVE ON past the mistake.

No need to punish yourself!
Jesus took our punishment and bore our
shortcomings.

Even after a firm correction,
the only voice coming from Him is still,
"Now rise up and walk!"

God is already for you...
Now YOU be for you!

Related Scriptures:

John 8:10-11 (NLT)
"Then Jesus stood up again and said to the woman, 'Where are your accusers? Didn't even one condemn you?' 'No, Lord,' she said. And Jesus said, 'Neither do I. **Go and sin no more.**'"

Romans 8:1 (NIV)
"Therefore, **there is now no condemnation** for those who are in Christ Jesus."

Matthew 11:28 (NLT)
"Then Jesus said, 'Come to me, all of you who are weary and carry heavy burdens, and I will give you rest.'"

Isaiah 55:4-6 (NIV)
"Surely **he took up our pain and bore our suffering**... he was crushed for our iniquities; **the punishment that brought us peace was on him...**"

PERSONAL NOTES:

Day 4
EVERYTHING I'M NOT

I thank God for everything I am…
but I'm just as thankful for everything I am NOT.

On the broad scale of things, it's only a few gifts
and talents we've each been given.

You will absolutely THRIVE when you FIND and
STAY in what God has graced you to do.

Learn how to utilize others around you and let them
utilize your strengths as well!

There is no need to cross over and try to be
something you're not or do something you hate and
have NO GRACE to do.

Realize that God uses other people in our lives to
bring COMPLETION.

Be thankful for others' strengths while continuing
to stay locked into your own sweet spot.

-

Self-Reflective Questions:
*What are some areas that I'm needlessly suffering in and can
begin to delegate?*

*What areas bring me the most joy and excitement in life, and how
can I keep myself in that sweet spot more often?*

Related Scriptures:

1 Corinthians 12:12 (NIV)
"For just as the body is one and has many members, and **all the members of the body,** though many, **are one body**, so it is with Christ."

Psalms 133:1,3 (NIV)
"How good and pleasant it is when God's people live **together in unity... for there, the LORD bestows his blessing**, even life forevermore."

Philippines 3:13,14 (KJV)
"**This one thing I do,** forgetting those things which are behind, and reaching forth unto those things which are before, **I press toward the mark...**"

PERSONAL NOTES:

Day 5
NO THANKS

Most of us need to practice two words:
"No thanks."

There's no need to justify your decisions.

Break the need to sugarcoat anything.

Sugar covers things that are not tasteful, but that's
not YOU. You're a lil sweetheart!

You can still be polite yet firm in your choices.

Whether 'yes' or 'no,' remove the pressure to prove
anything past that.

When explaining yourself, you'll usually find things
blown out of proportion and can easily slip into
lying—for LITERALLY NO REASON.

Go ahead and enjoy a life free from trying to
appease everyone and being overstretched with
unwanted commitments.

A simple "no thanks" will suffice.

Related Scriptures:

Matthew 5:37 (NKJV)
"But **let your 'Yes' be 'Yes,'** and your **'No,' 'No.'** For whatever is more than these is from the evil one."

James 1:8 (KJV)
"A double-minded man is unstable in all his ways."

Galatians 1:10 (ESV)
"**For am I now seeking the approval of man, or of God?** Or am I trying to please man? If I were still trying to please man, I would not be a servant of Christ."

Proverbs 12:23 (ESV)
"A prudent man conceals knowledge, but the heart of fools proclaims folly."

PERSONAL NOTES:

Day 6
STRETCH

Stretch now so you don't tear later.

God-given opportunities are like riding a wave.
You need to stay relaxed and flexible.

Be ready to go with the flow because when God's
timing hits, it happens FAST!

When expansion comes, you can quickly go from
feeling like a senior classman to the little freshman
in the room.

Prepare NOW for the new environment.

It doesn't need to be extreme; just make a conscious
decision to hear, do, and be around things that will
expand and stretch you in new ways.

How do you expect to grow if you only stick with
what you're already familiar and comfortable with?

-

Self-Reflective Questions:

*How can I purposefully stretch and expand today to further
prepare for where I believe God is taking me?*

Related Scriptures:

Ezekiel 11:19 (NLT)
"And I will give them singleness of heart and put a new spirit within them. I will take away their **stony, stubborn heart** and give them a **tender, responsive heart.**"

Matthew 9:17 (NLT)
"And no one puts new wine into old wineskins. **The old skins would burst from the pressure**, spilling the wine and ruining the skins. New wine is stored in new wineskins so that both are preserved."

Isaiah 52:2 (NIV)
"**Enlarge** the place of your tent, **stretch** your tent curtains wide, do not hold back; **lengthen** your cords, **strengthen** your stakes..."

PERSONAL NOTES:

Day 7
ONLY YOUR BEST

"Enlarge...
Build an addition...
Spread out...
Spare no expense...
You will soon be bursting at the seams" Isaiah 54:2
(NLT).

With God on your side, there is no reason to fear
or give any thought to shortage or the possibility of
running out!

The only thing you cannot afford is
WITHHOLDING your absolute best today.

Get your BEST nets ready.
Get every little detail in place for an "overwhelming
haul of fish." (Luke 5:4-7)

If it's not your best, the nets will break, and the full
potential of the opportunity will be missed.
ALL OF YOU is required to fully receive God's
best!

-

Self-Reflective Questions:
Are there any areas I am withholding giving my absolute best?

*What practical steps can I take to build out and expand in new
ways that I know the Holy Spirit is leading me to?*

Related Scriptures:

Isaiah 54:2,3 (NLT)
"Enlarge your house; build an addition. **Spread out your home, and spare no expense! For you will soon be bursting at the seams.**"

Luke 5:4-7 (NIV)
"...he said to Simon, 'Put out into deep water, and **let down the nets for a catch.**' ... When they had done so, **they caught such a large number of fish that their nets began to break.** So they signaled their partners in the other boat to come and help them, and **they came and filled both boats so full that they began to sink.**"

PERSONAL NOTES:

Day 8
EQUIPPED FOR CONFRONTATION

Being "more than a conqueror" means you are built and equipped for CONFRONTATION.

But instead of blowing off the hinges emotionally, you can rely on the Holy Spirit to fill your mouth with the right words at the right time.

The primary key to keeping your cool is to remain in LOVE and keep your heart set on the Holy Spirit inside you!

As you cultivate an intimate relationship with God, leaning on Him in challenging situations will get easier.

And just like King David, when the confrontation comes, you can confidently release the rock (aka the RIGHT words) exactly where it needs to hit...

The HEART of the problem.

Related Scriptures:

Mark 13:11 (ESV)
"And when they bring you to trial and deliver you over, **do not be anxious beforehand what you are to say**, but say whatever is given you in that hour, **for it is not you who speak, but the Holy Spirit.**"

1 Samuel 17: 45-48 (NIV)
"David **said to the Philistine**, "You come against me with sword and spear and javelin, **but I come against you** in the name of the Lord Almighty... This day the Lord will deliver you into my hands, and I'll strike you down and cut off your head... As the Philistine moved closer to attack him, **David ran quickly toward the battle line to meet him.** Reaching into his bag and taking out a stone, he slung it and struck the Philistine on the forehead. The stone sank into his forehead, and he fell facedown on the ground."

PERSONAL NOTES:

Day 9
A TRUE FATHER

The prodigal son would have settled to return as a servant, but the Father accepted him back as a son, placing a ring on his finger and dressing him in the finest robe without hesitation.

Essentially, the Father expressed, "Despite a betrayal, you're still a part of this family. There's blood in your veins that still makes you mine."

It's comforting to know your family status isn't up for grabs.

You won't live a life of insecurity when your heart is SECURE in this divine family structure.

The Father displays an unconditional love we rarely see in our performance-based society that will withdraw goodness until performance is up to par.

That's simply not the nature of a true father. Whether you 'feel it' or not, say it aloud for your ears to hear:
"I belong to MY Heavenly Father because He has decided to FIRST love ME."

We are not orphans. We're not even servants. We are sons/daughters of The Most High.

Related Scriptures:

1 John 4:19 (NIV)
"We love because **he first loved us**."

Luke 15:18-23 (NIV)
"I will set out and go back to my father and say to him: 'Father, I have sinned against heaven and against you. I am no longer worthy to be called your son; make me like one of your hired servants.' So he got up and went to his father.

"But while he was still a long way off, his father saw him and was filled with compassion for him; he ran to his son, threw his arms around him, and kissed him.
"The son said to him, 'Father, I have sinned against heaven and against you. I am no longer worthy to be called your son.'

"But the father said to his servants, 'Quick! Bring the best robe and put it on him. Put a ring on his finger and sandals on his feet. Bring the fattened calf and kill it. Let's have a feast and celebrate. For this son of mine was dead and is alive again; he was lost and is found.' So they began to celebrate."

1 John 3:1 (NIV)
"See what great love the Father has lavished on us, that we should be **called children of God**! And that is what we are."

PERSONAL NOTES:

Day 10
YOUR STORY

This is YOUR story now!

If you feel lonely… it's ok!
You're walking out your own story now!

If you think, "How is God going to come through?" That's an amazing moment because this is finally YOUR story playing out.

It's a lengthy process when you are the one living through it. You can't just flip the page for an immediate answer, like when reading someone else's story.

Understand that God is taking you from a place of second-hand information into first-hand experience.

You will no longer tell stories of what God did for others or only share someone else's revelation.

You will now begin to carry greater authority and weight on YOUR words.

There will be a red-hot fire when you share your personal testimony and have walked things out for yourself!

Related Scriptures:

Job 42:5 (NLT)
"I had only heard about you before, **but now I have seen you with my own eyes.**"

James 1:2-4 (NASB)
"Consider it all joy, my brethren, when you encounter various trials, knowing that the testing of your faith produces endurance. And **let endurance have its perfect result, so that you may be perfect and complete, lacking in nothing.**"

Revelation 12:11 (KJV)
"And they overcame him by the blood of the Lamb, **and by the word of their testimony ...**"

Psalms 34:4-8 (NIV)
"I sought the Lord, and he answered me; **he delivered me from all my fears. Those who look to him are radiant;** their faces are never covered with shame... **Taste and see that the Lord is good; blessed is the one who takes refuge in him.**"

Psalms 9:1 (NIV)
"I will give thanks to you, LORD, with all my heart; **I will tell of all your wonderful deeds.**"

PERSONAL NOTES:

Day 11
LOVE WILL GO TO WAR

Love will unlock the warrior in you.

"If you want to unleash 'mama bear,' touch mama's children!"

Why?
Love is a protector.
It demands the swift removal of danger or the agent of harm.

Don't believe love is docile or dormant.

It's an attempt to keep the TRUE champion out of the ring so the loser can win by default.

And by true champion... I mean YOU!

Prepare for a fire in your heart that will make the devil WISH he had never crossed the line with you.

It's time to SHOW UP for those you love and release the warrior IN YOU!

Related Scriptures:

Psalms 45:3,4 (NIV)
"**Gird your sword on your side, you mighty one**; clothe yourself with splendor and majesty. In your majesty, **ride forth victoriously in the cause of truth, humility, and justice; let your right hand achieve awesome deeds.**"

Isaiah 42:13 (NIV)
"The LORD will **march out like a champion; like a warrior**, he will stir up his zeal; **with a shout, he will raise the battle cry and triumph over his enemies.**"

Colossians 2:15 (NKJV)
"**Having disarmed principalities and powers**, He made a public spectacle of them, **triumphing over them in it.**"

Psalm 105:14,15 (NLT)
"Yet **he did not let anyone oppress them**. He warned kings on their behalf: "**Do not touch my chosen people, and do not hurt my prophets.**"

PERSONAL NOTES:

Day 12
THOSE WHO HAVE GONE BEFORE YOU

Sometimes, you won't realize how GOOD you have it until you truly understand how BAD it SHOULD have been.

It's too easy to reap the benefits of others who have gone before us and take what they've done for granted.

Don't waste what's been passed down to you!

It not only COULD be worse...
It SHOULD have been worse if God hadn't stepped in and intervened.

God has inspired generations before you to lay the groundwork that has created a better path for you to walk on.

Honor those who have paved the way for you to go where they could have never gone!

Their ceiling has now become your floor.

This came at a great price.
Don't squander it!

Related Scriptures:

Hebrews 12:1 (NIV)
"Therefore, since we are surrounded by such a **great cloud of witnesses,** let us throw off everything that hinders and the sin that so easily entangles. And let us run with perseverance the race marked out for us."

1 Timothy 5:17 (ESV)
"Let the elders who rule well be considered worthy of double honor."

Hebrews 13:7 (ESV)
"Remember your leaders, those who spoke to you the word of God. Consider the outcome of their way of life, and imitate their faith."

2 Timothy 1:5 (ESV)
"I am reminded of your sincere faith, **a faith that dwelt first in your grandmother** Lois **and your mother** Eunice and now, I am sure, **dwells in you as well.**"

PERSONAL NOTES:

Day 13
DIG

New is fun, but am I maximizing what I currently have?

Am I developing what God has given me to its fullest possible potential?

Keep working with what you have until you see it FULLY develop!

We tend to search for new things to keep ourselves excited.

However, like drilling for oil, sometimes we must DIG IN to find the newness and excitement we seek.

If you reach too broad, you'll spread thin, but if you drill down deeper, you'll hit NEW OIL!

I'm telling you... repetition is a powerful tool THAT MOST are underestimating!

DIG and watch how it will excite and even surprise YOU!

Related Scriptures:

Proverbs 12:24 (ESV)
"The hand of the diligent will rule, while the slothful will be put to forced labor."

Galatians 6:9 (ESV)
"And let us not grow weary of doing good, for in due season we will reap if we do not give up."

Proverbs 4:23 (NIV)
"Above all else, guard your heart, for everything you do flows from it."

John 7:38 (NIV)
"Whoever believes in me, as Scripture has said, **rivers of living water will flow from within them.**"

PERSONAL NOTES:

Day 14
ABSOLUTE INDEPENDENCE

Love allows absolute independence.
With total independence comes the option of
rebellion.

Love gave an angel, Lucifer, extreme beauty,
extraordinary musical ability, and influence.

Then, that angel decided to rebel.

Love gave a man, Adam, dominion on earth and
cultivated daily fellowship...
yet that man rebelled as well.

Isn't it interesting how God allowed these choices
to be made without interference?

The choices you make today carry more weight
than you've probably realized.

When God says, "TAKE HEED!"
Pay attention because your cooperation, or lack
thereof, will create a much more significant ripple
effect than you think.

Related Scriptures:

Galatians 6:7 (ESV)
"Do not be deceived: God is not mocked, for whatever one sows, that will he also reap."

Psalms 8:4-6 (NLT)
"What are mere mortals that you should think about them, human beings that you should care for them? Yet you made them only a little lower than God and crowned them with glory and honor. **You gave them charge of everything you made, putting all things under their authority.**"

Luke 10:19 (ESV)
"And he said to them, "I saw Satan fall like lightning from heaven. Behold, **I have given you authority** to tread on serpents and scorpions and over all the power of the enemy, and nothing shall hurt you."

PERSONAL NOTES:

Day 15
THE PROPOSAL

The Bridegroom has already made His decision.
Before you loved Him, He first loved you.

A covenant exchange has taken place.

But just like any wedding day, it will require
preparation and a separation process.

Do you realize God has deemed you special and
separated you unto Himself?

This truth remains despite any negative things
spoken over you to make you feel common or
unwanted.

Can God have permission to set you into your
special purpose?

If your answer is "Yes, I do,"
then you've just said yes to leaving a life of common
use for an EXTRAORDINARY purpose when all
is said and done.

Related Scriptures:

Revelation 19:8 (ESV)
"Let us rejoice and exult and give him the glory, for the marriage of the Lamb has come, and his Bride has made herself ready; it was granted her to clothe herself with fine linen, **bright and pure.**"

1 Corinthians 6:11 (CSB)
"And some of you used to be like this. **But you were washed, you were sanctified, you were justified** in the name of the Lord Jesus Christ and by the Spirit of our God."

2 Timothy 2:20-21(CSB)
"Now in a large house, there are not only gold and silver bowls, but also those of wood and earthenware, **some for special use, some for ordinary.** So if anyone purifies himself from these things, he will be a special instrument, set apart, useful to the Master, prepared for every good work."

PERSONAL NOTES:

Day 16
THE WHAT AND THE HOW

It's just as important to figure out 'HOW' God wants something to happen as it is 'WHAT' He wants to happen.

Most of the time, we receive the 'WHAT' and then think God's sending us out from there to do it ourselves.

Keep God in the driver's seat.

He who showed you 'WHAT' to do will also show you 'HOW' to do it.

"He who BEGAN this good work in you will also bring it to COMPLETION" (Philippians 1:6).

God doesn't send you out alone.
He is with you and guiding you every step of the way!

Keep all of the weight on God's shoulders and watch Him handle your situation better than you or anyone else could.

Related Scriptures:

Proverbs 16:9 (NKJ)
"A man's heart plans his way, but **the Lord directs his steps.**"

Philippians 1:6 (ESV)
"" am sure of this: that **he who started a good work in you will carry it on to completion** until the day of Christ Jesus."

Proverbs 3:5,6 (NIV)
"Trust in the LORD with all your heart and **lean not on your own understanding; in all your ways submit to him, and he will make your paths straight.**"

PERSONAL NOTES:

Day 17
LEAVING THE NINETY-NINE

You have a God-given assignment on the earth. It has everything to do with being a solution to a problem.

You carry an answer that someone desperately needs.

The temptation is to withhold your gift until your 'crowd' is big enough.

Instead, be quick to leave the crowd in order to reach the one.

There is that one person who desperately needs the gift that you carry.

Be willing to release what's in you now with absolutely EVERYTHING YOU HAVE, even if it is just for one person.

Don't allow numbers to manipulate your outflow and effort. As freely as you receive, freely give!

Related Scriptures:

Matthew 18:12 (NIV)
"What do you think? If a man owns a hundred sheep, and one of them wanders away, will he not leave the ninety-nine on the hills and go to **look for the one that wandered off.**"

Matthew 10:8 (NIV)
"Freely you have received; freely give."

1 Peter 5:6 (NIV)
"Humble yourselves, therefore, under God's mighty hand, that he may lift you up in due time."

Psalms 75:6,7 (KJV)
"For promotion cometh neither from the east, nor from the west, nor from the south. But God is the judge: he putteth down one, and setteth up another."

Proverbs 11:25 (BSB)
"A generous soul will prosper, and he who refreshes others will himself be refreshed."

PERSONAL NOTES:

Day 18
RISE AND CONQUER

What if, instead of being delivered out of the problem, you outgrow the problem itself?

If a school bully shows up and you keep asking to transfer to another school, you get a quick fix, but not a true solution.

If you grow bigger than the problem, now you can spearhead it. The problem can no longer manhandle you like it used to!

YOU can now take control of your environment, plus you are able to help deliver OTHERS as well.

This is all a roundabout way of describing what it looks like to be 'MORE than a conqueror.'

You have conquered, and you're now equipped to help those around you win their battles as well.

Today is an excellent day to RISE UP and CONQUER!

Related Scriptures:

Isaiah 54:17 (NLT)
"No weapon turned against you will succeed. You will silence every voice raised up to accuse you. These benefits are enjoyed by the servants of the LORD..."

Romans 8:37 (NKJV)
"Yet in all these things, **we are more than conquerors through Him** who loved us."

James 4:7 (ESV)
"Submit yourselves therefore to God. **Resist the devil, and he will flee from you.**"

Psalms 45:3,4 (NIV)
"Gird your sword on your side, you mighty one; clothe yourself with splendor and majesty. In your majesty, **ride forth victoriously in the cause of truth, humility, and justice; let your right hand achieve awesome deeds."**

PERSONAL NOTES:

Day 19
MULTIPLE ROUNDS

Some victories require multiple rounds and cycles of 'going through it.'

You thought you were past this, but when the rubber met the road, you weren't quite as strong or resolved as you thought.

IT'S OK!
Each cycle is still working something out.

Agreeing with a concept is much different from ingesting it until you can fully function in it.

Testing is the one thing that will let you know if what you may AGREE with is actually INSIDE of you!

Refuse to throw in the towel and give up.

Don't discount the God who supernaturally dissolves problems.

Trust that by doing the right thing when nothing looks different, you're simultaneously giving God permission to DISSOLVE what otherwise would have hassled you your whole life.

Related Scriptures:

Galatians 6:9 (NKJV)
"And let us not grow weary while doing good, for in due season **we shall reap if we do not lose heart.**"

Isaiah 43:19 (NIV)
"See, I am doing a new thing! Now it springs up; do you not perceive it? **I am making a way in the wilderness and streams in the wasteland.**"

1 Corinthians 3:13 (NIV)
"Their work will be shown for what it is because the Day will bring it to light. **It will be revealed with fire, and the fire will test the quality of each person's work.**"

James 1:2-4 (ESV)
"Count it all joy, my brothers, when you meet trials of various kinds, for you know that **the testing of your faith produces steadfastness**. And **let steadfastness have its full effect,** that you may be **perfect and complete,** lacking in nothing."

PERSONAL NOTES:

Day 20
OWNERSHIP

Ownership carries an entirely different attitude.

It can seem aggressive at first, but something clicks
into gear when you realize,
"This belongs to me."

The days of continually doing without will end
when you fully see it; "I have every right to be here
and have this."

An owner's attitude is entirely different from a hired
hand.

You carry a sense of command and walk with
authority that will set things into place.

A healthy anger will ignite when you truly begin to
see yourself as THE OWNER of what God says
ALREADY BELONGS to you.

It should get you upset that the ONLY reason you
have 'gone without' is because you were sold a lie
that kept you settling for leftovers when God had a
whole banquet spread out with YOUR NAME
written on it!

Related Scriptures:

Genesis 1:28 (AMPC)
"And God blessed them and said to them, Be fruitful, multiply, and fill the earth, and subdue it [using all its vast resources in the service of God and man]; and **have dominion...**"

Deuteronomy 1:8 (NIV)
"See, I have given you this land. Go in and take possession of the land the LORD swore he would give to your fathers."

Philippians 4:13 (NKJV)
"I can do all things through Christ who strengthens me."

Psalms 8:6 (NLT)
"You gave them **charge of everything you made, putting all things under their authority.**"

Joshua 1:3-6 (NIV)
"**I will give you every place where you set your foot**, as I promised Moses... **No one will be able to stand against you all the days of your life**. As I was with Moses, so I will be with you; I will never leave you nor forsake you. **Be strong and courageous...**"

PERSONAL NOTES:

Day 21
SURRENDERING CONTROL

We tend to be comfortable in a car (in control) and more fearful in a plane (surrendering control).

Yet the plane is statistically much safer and obviously much faster!

In the same way, there are heights we can go that will ONLY come in surrender.

You have a firm grip on everything in the shallows, but you're limited there.

In the 'deep,' you have to surrender a degree of control, but that's also where all the God-sized opportunities are.

If you've prayed for a bigger opportunity, don't back down now!

Especially when Jesus is telling YOU, "Launch out into the deep!"

Related Scriptures:

Mark 35:6 (ESV)
"Do not fear, only believe."

Matthew 10:39 (ESV)
"Whoever finds his life will lose it, and whoever loses his life for my sake will find it. **If you cling to your life, you will lose it; but if you give up your life for me, you will find it.**"

Hebrews 11:6 (NIV)
"And without faith, it is impossible to please God."

Luke 5:4-6 (BSB)
"He said to Simon, '**Put out into deep water and let down your nets for a catch.**' 'Master,' Simon replied, 'we have worked hard all night without catching anything. **But because You say so, I will let down the nets.**' When they had done so, **they caught such a large number of fish that their nets began to tear.**"

PERSONAL NOTES:

Day 22
THE UNKNOWN

The unknown will never be comfortable.
It's pure trust being exercised like a muscle.

God loves 'step-by-step' instruction.
So, it's OK to not have the complete picture yet.

If you don't know, you don't know.
Remain honest.

To pretend will only muddy the waters.

God WILL reveal things at the right time, and they
will be so obvious you can't miss them.

"There is nothing covered up that will not be
revealed, and hidden that will not be known" (Luke
12:2).

For now, enjoy today's journey, knowing that God
WILL REVEAL the following steps when you
arrive.

Daily Sparks Vol. 1

Related Scriptures:

John 16:13 (ESV)
"When the Spirit of truth comes, **he will guide you into all the truth**, for he will not speak on his own authority, but whatever he hears he will speak, and he will declare to you the **things that are to come**."

"...he will tell you what is yet to come." (NIV)
"...he will tell you about the future." (NLT)

Psalms 119:105 (NLT)
"Your word is a lamp to guide my feet and a light for my path."

Proverbs 4:18 (NIV)
"The path of the righteous is like the morning sun, shining ever brighter till the full light of day."

Luke 12:2 (NIV)
"There is nothing concealed that will not be disclosed, or **hidden that will not be made known**."

Matthew 6:31-33 (NLT)
"So **don't worry about these things**... These things dominate the thoughts of unbelievers, but your heavenly Father already knows all your needs. **Seek the Kingdom of God above all else,** and live righteously, and **he will give you everything you need**."

PERSONAL NOTES:

44

Day 23
THE APPOINTMENT IS SET

We tend to get discouraged by the time things may take, yet NOTHING God has spoken to you has changed or diminished.

Think about it.
God hasn't changed.
His Word concerning you hasn't changed.

The one variable in this equation that is changing is YOU.

Time is on your side.
Use this time to grow and prepare.

Your God-given appointment is set!

Many people don't arrive at their end destination because time defeats them, but that's NOT YOU!

The main separator will be that you've decided to KEEP SHOWING UP and, in due season, saw God's promises come to pass!

Remember, the appointment is SET.
Just stay on course!

Related Scriptures:

Psalms 102:13 (NKJV)
"You will arise *and* have mercy on Zion; For the time to favor her, **Yes, the set time, has come.**"

Galatians 6:9 (NIV)
"Let us not become weary of doing good, **for at the proper time we will reap a harvest if we do not give up.**"

Numbers 23:19 (ESV)
"**God is not man, that he should lie**, or a son of man, that he should change his mind. Has he said, and **will he not do it?** Or has he spoken, and **will he not fulfill it?**"

1 Peter 5:6 (NLT)
"So humble yourselves under the mighty power of God, and **at the right time he will lift you up in honor.**"

Ephesians 6:13,14 (NIV)
"...and after you have done everything, to stand. Stand firm then..."

PERSONAL NOTES:

Day 24
REFUSE TO FEED ON DAILY DISAPPOINTMENTS

Refuse to feed on daily disappointing reminders!

You have an appointment with success IF you'll turn your focus.

Instead of continually setting the thing that is discouraging you as the focus, shift your focus to the WISDOM required to get you and KEEP you up and out of these recurring problems.

Allow the Lord to put His hands on things and be willing to adjust whatever He shows you along the way.

Look for God to highlight a word or scripture for you to hold on to. And once you have it, wage war with it daily by SPEAKING IT OUT LOUD!

Yes, it can take time and patience.
But that's ok; we are in this for the long haul!

-

Self-Reflective Questions:
Is there anything around me feeding disappointment and deflating me that I can remove?

What can I add to my day to increase my passion and inspiration?

Related Scriptures:

Colossians 3:2 (NIV)
"**Set your minds on things above**, not on earthly things."

Philippians 4:8-9 (KJV)
"Whatsoever things are true, whatsoever things are honest, whatsoever things are just, whatsoever things are pure, whatsoever things are lovely, whatsoever things are of good report; if there be any virtue, and if there be any praise, **think on these things**."

Proverbs 24:3 (NKJV)
"Through wisdom, a house is built, and by understanding, it is established."

Proverbs 24:3 (AMP)
"Through [skillful and godly] wisdom **a house [a life, a home, a family] is built, And by understanding it is established [on a sound and good foundation].**"

PERSONAL NOTES:

Day 25
SURPRISINGLY GOOD

If you could read your entire story now, you would
see how 'unfair' it was...
But for your good!

Know that God is stacking things in your favor as
you keep Him first.

Others could say, "God, that's cheating!"
But His reply would be, "No, that's My favor and
reward to My faithful ones."

If you're tempted to quit, DON'T!
Stay faithful!

As long as you stay plugged into the things of God,
He is CONSTANTLY working things out behind
the scenes. (God doesn't sleep!)

You will see how God has stacked things in your
favor the further down the road you travel.

For now, know that The Author of your life still has
the pen in His hand.

Give Him thanks today for ALL the good things
He has hand-written into YOUR STORY!

Related Scriptures:

1 Chronicles 17:16-17 (NIV)
"Then King David went in and sat before the LORD, and he said: **"Who am I, LORD God, and what is my family, that you have brought me this far?** And as if this were not enough in your sight, my God, you have spoken about the future of the house of your servant. **You, LORD God, have looked on me as though I were the most exalted of men.**"

Psalms 5:12 (NIV)
"Surely, Lord, you bless the righteous; **you surround them with your favor** as with a shield."

Proverbs 3:1-4 (ESV)
"Let not steadfast love and faithfulness forsake you; bind them around your neck; write them on the tablet of your heart. So you will find favor and good success in the sight of God and man."

Psalms 84:11 (ESV)
"For the Lord God is a sun and shield; the Lord bestows favor and honor. **No good thing does he withhold from those who walk uprightly.**"

PERSONAL NOTES:

Day 26
AN UNBROKEN FLOW

Once you can SEE something on the inside, it's just a matter of time until it shows up on the outside.

It may take years to truly see a clear image in your heart, but one day, it will 'click' if you just stick with it.

"A house divided cannot stand" (Matthew 12:25). This would also mean that a house that is unified and undivided CANNOT BE broken.

Creativity, ingenuity, and solutions will FLOW once your inner image gets clear and defined!

The flow will come at such a rate that you can barely even keep up.

It starts in the 'home of YOU'!

Allow God to make you crystal clear and singular (spirit, soul, and body) so that you can fully flow into who He's made you to be...

UNHINDERED and UNBROKEN.

Related Scriptures:

Genesis 11:6 (KJV)
"Behold, the people *is* one, and they have all one language; and this they begin to do: and now **nothing will be restrained from them, which they have imagined to do.**"

Mark 3:24,25 (BSB)
"If a kingdom is divided against itself, it cannot stand. And **if a house is divided against itself, it cannot stand.**"

Proverbs 4:23 (NIV)
"Above all else, guard your heart, for everything you do flows from it."

John 7:38 (NIV)
"Whoever believes in me, as Scripture has said, **rivers of living water will flow from within them.**"

Exodus 31:3 (NLT)
"**I have filled him with the Spirit of God, giving him great wisdom, ability, and expertise** in all kinds of crafts."

PERSONAL NOTES:

Day 27
SLOW AND STEADY

Pace yourself.
Take time to rest and recharge.

We've all likely heard it and need to hear it again:
"Life is not a sprint; it's a MARATHON!"

So why not keep things as fun as possible?

Ask yourself, "Where is my current level of
enjoyment from day to day?"

It's the secret to getting where you want to go and
staying there long-term.

The length of time won't matter once you've
learned how to enjoy the process.

And rather than a short burst of faith, you'll find
the calmness that's only found in a day-in and
day-out LIFE of faith.

It's not a sprint. It's not a giant leap.
It's just incremental steps as we WALK by faith
each and every day.

Related Scriptures:

2 Corinthians 5:7 (ESV)
"We **walk by faith**, not by sight."

Proverbs 13:11 (NKJV)
"Wealth gained hastily will dwindle, but whoever gathers **little by little will increase it**."

Proverbs 13:11 (NLT)
"Wealth from **get-rich-quick schemes quickly disappears**; wealth from hard work **grows over time**."

Isaiah 40:31 (KJV)
"They that wait upon the LORD shall renew their strength; they shall mount up with wings as eagles; **they shall run, and not be weary; and they shall walk, and not faint**."

Hebrews 12:1 (NLT)
"Let us strip off every weight that slows us down, especially the sin that so easily trips us up. And **let us run with endurance the race God has set before us**."

PERSONAL NOTES:

Day 28
A BLANK CANVAS

See the possibilities of what CAN BE instead of what currently is.

"I make a pathway through the wilderness. I create rivers in dry wastelands so that My people may be refreshed" (Isaiah 43:19, 20).

God, the Creator, loves to work with a canvas that seems dry and desolate to create something beautiful.

'Nothing' is actually a great start for 'something.'

What the world deems desolate and abandoned, God calls a blank canvas and thinks,
"Let's CREATE!"

Change your perspective from...
"There's nothing here."
to
"I've just stepped into endless creative possibilities!"

God always has a solution, even if the solution is to create SOMETHING out of NOTHING.

Related Scriptures:

Isaiah 43:18,19 (NIV)
"Forget the former things; do not dwell on the past. **See, I am doing a new thing!** Now it springs up; do you not perceive it? **I am making a way in the wilderness and streams in the wasteland.**"

Romans 4:17 (NLT)
"Abraham believed in the God who brings the dead back to life and **who creates new things out of nothing.**"

"...who gives life to the dead and calls into existence the things that do not exist" (ESV).
"...the One giving life to the dead and calling into being the things not even existing" (BLB).

1 Corinthians 1:27-31 (NIV)
"But God chose the foolish things of the world to shame the wise; God chose the weak things of the world to shame the strong. God chose the lowly things of this world and the despised things—and the things that are not—to nullify the things that are, so that no one may boast before him."

PERSONAL NOTES:

Day 29
LIMITLESS

If you take the time to look at creation, it doesn't take long to see that The Creator is completely limitless and mind-bogglingly excessive.

When fear yells out, *"Lockdown!"*
make the conscious decision to OPEN UP all the more!

You don't have to play by others' self-imposed boundaries and limitations.

See beyond just you.
Don't sell God short of getting glory through you!

God is looking for someone to dream with His supply in mind.

If you only think within the confines of what you can do, then God is unnecessary in your life and dreams.

Freely dream and give GOD a job!

There is ALWAYS more when you serve a God who is completely LIMITLESS!

Related Scriptures:

Psalms 147:5 (MSG)
"Our Lord is great, **with limitless strength**; we'll never comprehend what he knows and does."

Matthew 19:26 (NIV)
"Jesus looked at them and said, 'With man this is impossible, but **with God all things are possible**.'"

Ephesians 3:20 (ESV)
"Now to him who is able to do **far more abundantly than all that we ask or think**, according to the power at work within us."

John 14:12 (NIV)
"Very truly I tell you, whoever believes in me will do the works I have been doing, and **they will do even greater things than these, because I am going to the Father**."

Luke 6:38 (NIV)
"Give, and it will be given to you. A good measure, pressed down, shaken together, and **running over, will be poured into your lap**. For with the measure you use, it will be measured to you."

PERSONAL NOTES:

Day 30
SUBTLE

'Subtle' is a powerful force.

We tend to underestimate our impact, but even seemingly small things are leaving a mark on the world around us.

It's when you DON'T realize someone is watching you that your actions are speaking louder than ever.

It's the subtle things you might not think mean much, but you're expressing genuine goodness and love… and it's affecting people in ways you don't realize!

It may seem minor or subtle, but GOD IS IN IT when genuine goodness is flowing out of your heart towards someone.

These are the seeds planted in the world all around you that will grow into oak trees later in life.

REFUSE to hold back the goodness in your heart. Your impact is more widespread and effective than you realize.

Related Scriptures:

Matthew 13:31,32 (ESV)
"The kingdom of heaven is like a grain of mustard seed that a man took and sowed in his field. It is **the smallest of all seeds**, but **when it has grown, it is larger than all the garden plants and becomes a tree** so that the birds of the air come and make nests in its branches."

John 15:12 (ESV)
"This is My commandment, that you love one another as I have loved you."

Galatians 6:10 (NLT)
"Therefore, whenever we have the opportunity, we should do good to everyone—especially to those in the family of faith."

Proverbs 3:27 (NIV)
"Do not withhold good from those to whom it is due, when it is in your power to act."

PERSONAL NOTES:

SALVATION PRAYER

If you've never officially made Jesus the Lord of your life, please take this opportunity to settle that once and for all. He is the one and only connection to God, The Father!

Go to sleep tonight in COMPLETE peace that all your sins are forgiven and that your eternity is secure... THEN wake up every morning to a fresh and thriving relationship with God!

"If you declare with your mouth, 'Jesus is Lord,' and believe in your heart that God raised him from the dead, you will be saved" Romans 10:9 (NIV).

It's that easy! People make it hard, but it's really not. Jesus did all the heavy lifting. We simply receive it by faith and enter into a NEW life in Christ.

Pray this prayer with me:
Father, I come to you in Jesus' name. I accept what Jesus has done on the cross and receive Him as Lord of my life. I repent of my sins and receive the cleansing power of Jesus. I make Heaven my home. Thank you for loving and saving me! In Jesus' name, I pray this. AMEN!

If you've prayed that prayer from the heart, WELCOME to the family of God! Continue to CULTIVATE and GROW your relationship with God every day like you did with this devotional!

ABOUT THE AUTHOR

Tyler Jaynes is a musician and singer-songwriter passionate about his relationship with God. This passion has culminated in his releasing two albums in the past decade and his beginning to author books.

He thrives in spontaneity and creativity. His authenticity is expressed through his distinguished style of music and writing.

Tyler is known for his laid-back and light-hearted personality with family and friends, yet he has a zeal and undeniable depth when it comes to the things of God.

TYLER JAYNES MUSIC

If you enjoyed Tyler's devotional, be sure to check out his music, which is available on all major music streaming platforms.

TylerJaynes.com

Connect with Tyler on social media:
Youtube: /tylerjaynesmusic
Facebook: /tylerjaynesmusic
Instagram: @tyler_jaynes

Made in the USA
Columbia, SC
17 January 2025

51943472R00039